a more perfect Union

The Journal Charles B. Wheeler Poetry Prize

a more perfect Union

Teri Ellen Cross Davis

MAD CREEK BOOKS, AN IMPRINT OF
THE OHIO STATE UNIVERSITY PRESS
COLUMBUS

Mad Creek Books, an imprint of The Ohio State University Press.

Library of Congress Cataloging-in-Publication Data
Names: Cross Davis, Teri Ellen, author.
Title: A more perfect Union / Teri Ellen Cross Davis.
Description: Columbus : Mad Creek Books, an imprint of The Ohio
    State University Press, [2021] | Summary: "Poems at once angry and
    tender explore motherhood, race, sexuality, and a Black woman's
    complicated relationship with her country"—Provided by publisher.
Identifiers: LCCN 2020030359 | ISBN 9780814257784 (paperback) |
    ISBN 081425778X (paperback) | ISBN 9780814280898 (ebook) | ISBN
    0814280897 (ebook)
Subjects: LCSH: American poetry—African American authors.
Classification: LCC PS3603.R6794 M67 2021 | DDC 811/.6—dc23
LC record available at https://lccn.loc.gov/2020030359

Cover design by Angela Moody
Text design by Juliet Williams
Type set in Adobe Palatino

*This collection is dedicated to my grandmother
Katie Mae "Ma," my husband, Hayes Davis,
(my first reader), the progeny Z & A, and
to all my born and found family.*

Contents

Acknowledgments   *ix*

PART I

The Goddess of Blood   3
Black Berries   5
A Black Woman Gets a Window Seat on Aer Lingus   7
The Goddess of Scars   8
Bad Girls Album Cover   9
White Barbie   10
3939 Strandhill Road, Cleveland, Ohio   11
The Goddess of Parenting   14
Co-sleeping   15
Baby Girl   16
Don't Act Like A   20
Keep   21
Knowledge of the Brown Body   22
Knuckle Head   23

PART II

The Goddess of Interracial Dating   27
Prince Album Cover   28
Houses of the Holy Led Zeppelin Album Cover   29
A Black Woman Learns Ireland's History by Bus   30
The First Gospel of Prince   32
Vous êtes ici   33
The Second Gospel of Prince   34

The Goddess of Lust   35
Her 21st Summer   36
The Third Gospel of Prince   38
The Goddess of Idolatry   39
Love Letter   41
"Don't Disturb This Groove"   42
Ode to Orgasms   43
Slow Drag   45
Escape Ladder   46

PART III

The Goddess of Anger   49
Lola Visits the Underworld   51
Backup (An Ode to Weathering)   52
When I Am the Only One in the Room   53
The Goddess of Cleaning   54
Partus sequitur ventrem   55
The Account of Katie Mae   57
The Goddess of the South   60
Thank You Jesus   62
Crescendo   63
This Poem Suggests Revolution   65
a more perfect Union   67

Notes   69

Acknowledgments

Thank you to the Virginia Center for the Creative Arts; Hedgebrook; the Community of Writers at Lake Tahoe, California; the Sustainable Arts Foundation; and the Freya Project for giving me space and support for the work in this collection. Thank you to the Black Ladies Brunch Collective: Saida Agostini, Anya Creightney, Celeste Doaks, Tafisha Edwards, and Katy Richey for their righteous support and friendship. Thank you to my monthly workshop—Abby Beckel, Michael Gushue, and Kim Roberts for keeping me honest and beholden to create new work. Thanks to Kathy Fagan, Forrest Gander, Jane Hirshfield, Linda Pastan, and Melissa Tuckey.

I am thankful to these journals, anthologies, and websites for publishing this work, some in earlier versions:

"Crescendo" and "Thank You Jesus," *Academy of American Poets*

"3939 Strandhill Road" and "White Barbie," *Beltway Poetry Quarterly*

"Don't Disturb This Groove," "Slow Drag," and "Ruminations on Prince B-Sides and Rarities, Part II," *Fledgling Rag*

"A Black Woman Learns Ireland's History by Bus" and
   "Back-Up (Ode to Weathering), *Figure 1*
"Thank You Jesus," *Harvard Review Online*
"The Goddess of Scars," *Kenyon Review*
"Escape Ladder," *Kestrel: A journal of literature and art*
"Ode to Orgasms," *Little Patuxent Review*
"This Poem Suggests Revolution," *Love's Executive Order*
"Co-sleeping," *Mom Egg Review*
"Knuckle Head," *North American Review*; and *FURIOUS FLOWER: Seeding the Future of African American Poetry*
"Prince Album Cover" and "Houses of the Holy album cover" *Not Without Our Laughter: an anthology of joy, laughter, and sexuality*
"A Black Woman Gets a Seat on Aer Lingus," *Pacifica Literary Review*
"The Goddess of Blood," *Pank: Health and Healing Folio*
"Don't Act Like A," *Poetry Ireland Review*
"Baby Girl," *Rape Can & Must End: Poems RaceBaitr.com*
"Partus Sequitur Ventrem" and "Keep," *Raising Mothers.com*
"Partus Sequitur Ventrem," *Rocked by the Waters: Poems of Motherhood*
"The Goddess of the South," *Rosebud Magazine #68*
"Crescendo," *Tin House*

Part I

The Goddess of Blood

Many pagans believed in the five sacred mysteries of blood:
birth, menarche, pregnancy and birthing, menopause, and death.

Birth
You rode in on your mother's
tidal prayer. I baptized you
in vernix and blood.

Menarche
I came to you again at ten—
such a rusty entrance, a door
swinging open. You stopped
diving into snow dunes long enough
to put on one of your aunt's pads
then head back out into the Cleveland night.

Soon after, my monthly visitations
held the fecund smell of ritual.
No perfume or pad could ever deny me.
Your prayers, dependable and mundane:
please, stop the cramps . . . but I packed white pants.
You would plead, I would do what I pleased—
mapping the universe within you.

Pregnancy and Birthing
After eight years of marriage
I swelled the fruit of you. Made
you spring. You bloomed like
Washington's magnolias,
laden with possibility—
the madder matter of me
folding and cleaving inside.

Months later, you blossomed a girl
child. Beatific in hematic glory, two
years later you produced a son. For
my sacrifice, a carmine current soaked
the delivery bed. Later, your breasts
welled up with sustenance, giving you a
taste of my power. Your prayers shined
with a new reverence. Bending down,
you would sniff your babies' crowns
looking for my scent.

Menopause
Decades later, you've come to value
my sanguine sovereignty. As I take
my slow exit—I have become
an ordering of the unpredictable.
At the midnight altar of your bed
I anoint you—rivulets of sweat running
down your softening body.

Death
And when death comes
will you be a wrung sponge?
Will you see how alive I made you?

Black Berries

Leave it to the seventy-year-old
Black woman, her honey skin
glowing, to tell me where
the best blackberries grow
on this island in the Puget Sound.

Reaching into the circular bushes
cautious of the cane's red thorns,
I hunt for the blackest berry.
A ripeness betrayed by fattened
drupelets, skin near bursting,
purple streaking my fingers
up to the elbows. Nature shows
her work, clusters on biennial vines.

Know the tender ones won't satisfy,
persist, let your fingertips stroke
the yielding weight of sweetness
a near-hidden whisper of a kiss,
blood berries, joyful and round
dappled in luster of late afternoon sun.

II. LIMERICK, IRELAND

The blacker the berry
the sweeter the juice,
I told my Irish friend,
his speckled hand reaching
deeper into a homegrown
bush of currants—searching
for the ripest for his Black
American guest. The young ones,

5

a blushed violet, bled streaks
on his cream fingers but he kept
pushing, past crimson, dark garnet,
until sweet midnight unveiled itself.

The intermittent sun shed ribbons
of yellow light over the River Shannon,
the swimming swans' tragedy
a sole surviving gosling
—all eclipsed by the black currant
its tender rupture
on the hilt of my tongue.

III. MOMBASA, KENYA

With long braids and dark skin
few knew I wasn't Kenyan.
Here, melanin was a blessing.
The batik bikini, baby oil,
equatorial sun—how Black
could I get? I never burned,

only burnished strains of buttermilk
blocking anything deeper. I could not
have done this in the States. I would never
call it "tanning," having never been tan.
But in Mombasa, drunk on a camel
crossing the spilling evening sand,
ocean surf, my cover band—
I chased my color, taunted it
to come out and play.

A Black Woman Gets a Window Seat on Aer Lingus

Enough Ireland.

For all your lush

effusion of color—

inside me blooms

a masochistic loneliness.

Give me the screws

I know best,

the policeman

quick to test

my *Yes, Sir*

as acidless.

Trigger the Midwest.

Never on the Bible

school test was this:

crucifixion kills, not nails

into feet or wrists

but the weight borne

upon the breast.

You suffocate slowly

in your own flesh.

As I return

to the upright cross

of the US,

I breathe easier,

I breathe less.

The Goddess of Scars

I mark you with melanin.
A crosshatch of collagen—
better the scar than the loss
of limb, better the clean line,
raised itch, festering wound
beckoning death.
My apostles: my keloids,
my atrophic, my contractures,
my hypertrophic response—
each a love I bear to the
mammal of you, the ruptured
vessel, the broken-in dermis.
Consider my evolution
a song to survival. Consider
cells my priests, their work
a ladder of prayer, each
stitch an epistle. I grieve
to see you separate from
your self. My atonement
is a bridge to build you back
together—while you can never
be born again, you can recover.
Each time I sign you, witness
the parable of action and
consequence. I do not think
you show enough reverence.
You were never meant
to be a smooth canvas
but a texture, a testament.
I bless you with a story
and each and every time
you live to tell the tale.

Bad Girls Album Cover

By the time I was seven, I knew I would like sex, knew
I would be good at it. I practiced lying on my back,

knees bent, hairless prepubescent folds angled up to the air.
I knew nothing of the actual act. The only penis I had ever seen

was by accident—opening the bathroom door on my father's
friend. But this was the time of Donna Summer. Under a

streetlamp's maraschino cherry glow, she posed—wet black
ringlets framed her light brown-sugared face, pouting lips

slick in shiny scarlet gloss, high heel perched on the lamp's base,
plunging the slit of her dress back to reveal a black lace stocking

a garter as garnish—so naughty, so beautiful. Why wouldn't I
want to be like her—up front about being wanted?

White Barbie

White Barbie's body fit easily
between two black iron railings—

no need for bondage. She was always
perfectly cast as a damsel in distress.

White Barbie in *The Sacrifice*
to Cookie Monster. White Barbie

stolen away by *The Handsome Thief.*
White Barbie discovered *On A Desert Island.*

Dressed well for her role, one shoulder bare,
a silver-column gown, heels flung during the struggle.

Sometimes she'd scream   faint
horror frozen on her painted face. Oh,

the monster would have her. The gown
would unsnap, shimmying down slim hips,

nippleless breasts, plastic cones in golden
afternoon light. A stark trail of blonde strands

hanging limply from Cookie Monster's maw of a mouth.
White Barbie—fragile, wanted, pretty—the best victim.

3939 Strandhill Road, Cleveland, Ohio

Like intruders, we tread cautiously
on the icy stone path around the house.

This is the landscape of my dreams.
The iron gate that safeguarded the patio?

Rusted and flaking to the ground. Creaking,
it acquiesces, announces our entry

to the empty yard behind us.
We peer through windows,

just like thieves forty-five years ago—
my grandfather finding their footsteps

in newly fallen snow. Now the windows
are striped with bars so we see nothing.

The boxy backyard that housed
my Barbie's adventures seems smaller,

tamer now. This was my father's home,
mine; now it's a listing in the paper.

My aunt still has keys. She takes us inside.
Under dust, a living room huddles.

Sunny tile in the kitchen clashes
against the black/white remodeling.

Upstairs in what was once
my parents' threshold,

my husband hunches
awkwardly to fit.

I lead him to my old room,
but it's no longer pink

shell and succor. A boy slept here.
I can tell. Still my lips spill

story after story, each nick, gouge, crayon-score
cracked walls echo back, more hollow

than before. I cannot paint the colors right.
Can't fill in the laughter, the security —

each name carved in wood on the bookcase.
Out front Mommy and I planted tulips;

red then yellow, until the squirrels
mixed them up. Thirty years later

only two survive, haggard and slumped,
punked by the longer, lingering winter.

Grandma's daylilies, her pride, wilt
in this nor'easter's grasp. My aunt

locks the door behind us. I'm not
sure it was good to say goodbye from

this close. Back in Maryland, the past
was pictures buried in a photo album.

Now I am deafened by the din of loss;
blinded by April snow. This was the first house

our family owned. My grandfather's trust
in land, finances—a safety net. Grief unravels

my tightrope. I rage at seeing the ground
rush up, my center of gravity gone.

The Goddess of Parenting

Pray to me and I give you a vagina
that feels like you birthed a bowling
ball. Squalling babes breaking buttons
on your blouse. Nipples torqued by
gums as hard as spines. You sucked
through with every spurt: the cream

and the hind. Pray to me for a moment
alone while hiding on the toilet, or when
you're automatically handed something,
pockets already full of snot rags, pills,
candy. Pray to me when you lock
the bedroom door for a quickie—
kneel, then remember when you
had time to play. Pray more and I'll

give you tempest-blown storms
from inarticulate shitting tyrants,
a full day of work followed by a long laundry
list in a cluttered home. Worship the walls
wounded with scribbles and gashes, banged
baby gates, black marks measuring how

they grow. Forget scraped knees, now
it's concussions. Pray after a few days
with no screens. You knew the end
result with that first kiss. There's a reason
why I blessed practice—made it bliss.
I'm not the Goddess for your rest,
you prayed for the title: *Mommy, Daddy,*
there is no riding the bench.

Co-sleeping

Years from now when they are teens,
out studying the art of lying,
I am told I will treasure
this imperfect sleep.

Two- and-four-year-old feet
in my back and stomach. Soft
bodies fattened by my milk, such
slight impressions they make

on a queen-sized mattress.
My weight, a well, sinks them
closer. I breathe in the stupor
of their sweet-rot breath—

my children are alive. I taste the words,
loll them in my mouth like a chewed
pacifier, each petite exhalation
secure knowledge. I swaddle this fact.

Fold it tight, tuck in its edges, wrap it again.
Alive, in this moment, on this night,
I—burrow in, knowing sleep won't come,
but curl around them, a shield, settled and still.

Baby Girl

January 2009, Monday night
When my firstborn came into this world,
my husband exclaimed *It's a girl!*—such glee.
I thought, *Oh shit, Freaknik!*
Please don't let her do that to me.
Implicit apology gushing down to the elbow of the moment.

Later I train her in dresses, skirts,
words like *pretty, eyelash, coquettish,* and *smile.*
Her biceps grow so large. I lace her with the barbs
most use to harm, but Mommy takes their sting away.

Amazon, my *big* girl
my *strong* girl my *smart* girl.

April 1995, Sunday night
Because she was small
she could fit in the window's
bay frame where she threatened to jump
if the frat boy didn't keep his hands off her.
She laughs when she remembers this moment.
Humor the filter over the terror, the tired.
It had been a long three days.

Friday day
Spring break—all the White kids
were at Florida beaches, the Black
kids in Atlanta for Freaknik.
Campus was a ghost town.
The three of them looked at each other
with a dream. Last-minute methods
of the poor and pretty are many.

Questionable decisions made quickly:
Cash: sixty dollars, one credit card,
a cousin rents them a car
but it can't go out of state.
Ok, bet.

Friday night
It wasn't the siren's cry that woke her—
the mixtape was too bumping for that—
but the red and blue swirling lights
bouncing off the backseat windows.
Seconds ago, she'd been asleep, now
a White cop had his gun unholstered
and pointed at her head, yelling
Get the fuck out the car!
Welcome to Tennessee.
Three skinny Black girls
on the side of a highway at
midnight, the driver's T-shirt torn.
What a threat to the man with the gun.

Friday night/Saturday morning
The Black bondsman
with kind eyes bails
the driver out,
but they gotta be back
on Monday for the hearing.

Saturday afternoon
A convertible Caddy
cruising Atlanta streets,
treetops filtering sunlight.
Blunts, burgers, brews
passed freely, Southern hospitality.

Saturday night
Black lace leotard,
no bra. She writes the night
in disappearing ink.
In his eyes, a sparkle.
Confidence? Cockiness?
Curly braids projecting
a framed innocence.
Funny how his hand
keeps appearing
on her waist.

Sunday night
The bondsman picks them up.
Drives them to the campus of
University of Tennessee,
Chattanooga. *These guys
can put you up for the night,* he says.

Questionable decisions made quickly:
Kappa Alpha Psi,
pretty boys and striped canes on one side.
Omegas Psi Phi,
Q's that just crossed on the other side.
Those Q's look like fun.

Questionable decisions made quickly:
Let's play Spades for shots!
With a new partner!
She wins twelve books in a row,
increasingly sober.
But the Q's ain't.
So, who really won?

Decisions to do sooner than later:
Call home.
They don't know
where she is.
She needs a bus ticket
back to school.

Places where guys hid:
Closets (2)
Under bed (2)

How many times were they chased through that small apartment?
Just one of them? Or all three of them?

What happened before she stood in the arched window threatening to jump?
He showed her his python.
He locked the door.
His hands followed her everywhere
until she was tired of squirming out of muscled arms,
tired of being on guard, tired of the laughing through her threats.
To be serious meant it was.

He said, *It's a girl!*
I'm a gaping portal
the doctor's trying to staunch.
My daughter is placed on my chest.
Her head cranes to the sound,
the smell of me. Consciousness
a black sheet fluttering.
Every muscle tried.
The world will want to wound her,
will want her bloodied lip and its kisses.
I've got to prepare her for both.

Don't Act Like A

On the train from Baltimore
a woman ignores her young son
until his boredom makes mischief fun
and her unengaged gaze narrows, sharpens,
before we all hear the slap followed by words
meant to bruise: *Don't act like a faggot.*
Maybe years later he will kiss a man
and taste despair, maybe years later
he will kick a man to hide his own fear.
Maybe none of these things will happen.
But my own silence is cultivated by years
of attempted interventions met with
blistering invectives, my own verbal fumbles
trying not to judge, while judging.
I wonder how long it will take
to embrace a masculinity not drenched
in cowardice, its stench as strong as semen.
I wonder how many years until we learn
not disgust, the instant flippant rebuke,
but the joy of a boy dancing
in his sister's princess dress, how the frills
flounce as he runs down the hall.
The pink spaghetti straps framing square
shoulders waiting to broaden and fill.

Keep

When it finally happened,
when the girl broke free,
pushed out, doctor
elbow-deep in me,
massaging a weeping
uterus—it would be weeks
later between diaper changes,
a hardened umbilicus fell.

Listless from lack of sleep
I missed its leap, sixty
centimeters of legacy
cut to a stump,
this physical keep—
my body's ancestral store,
snipped, shuttered, lost.

By the second child, a boy,
I knew. He would be the last.
So, I kept a bloodshot eye
on the striated yellow
hardening knot,
this sieve, this tether,
triad of blood vessels.
How crucial this lifeline
from fetus to placenta to me,
how essential I *was*
each *breath,*
each *bite,*
until I was *not.*

Knowledge of the Brown Body

After "Harriet Tubman is a Lesbian" by Saida Agostini

If Harriet Tubman had been a lesbian
I would know the brown body had been
valued outside of chattel, to the point of risk.
I would know an ebony nipple spoke its hushed
volumes from inside another sweet brown mouth,
eager to know its secrets. I would know a brown
belly had been showered with a free tongue's pulsing
intention. I would know the brown hips of a woman
were stolen back for freedom's sake. I would know
that brown thigh's thunder was enough to make a woman walk
into the abyss of the deep South and come out clapping,
on fire with black love. I would know that this body I own
had once been coveted for its sake and its sake alone.
How sacred I could hold that knowledge, I could palm it,
my fingers deep inside the agent that helped break
the back of the Confederacy.

Knuckle Head

My son's head is a fist
rapping against the door of the world.
For now, it's dressers, kitchen islands,

dining room tables that coax his clumsy,
creating small molehills of hurt breaching
the surface. The ice pack,

a cold kiss to lessen the blow equals
a frigid intrusion; a boy cannot be a boy
with all this mothering getting in the way.

Sometimes the floor plays accomplice
snagging an ankle, elbow, top lip to swell.
Other times it's a tantrum, when he spills his limbs

onto the hardwood, frenzied then limp with anger,
tongue clotted with frustration,
a splay of two-year-old emotion voiced in one winding wail.

My son cannot continue this path. Black boys
can't lose control at twelve, eighteen, even forty-three.
They don't get *do-overs.*

So, I let him flail about now,
let him run headfirst into the wall,
learn how unyielding perceptions can be.

Bear the bruising now, before he grows,
enters a world too eager to spill his blood,
too blind to how red it is.

Part II

The Goddess of Interracial Dating

I whisper *caramel*
to his refined
white sugar dreams,
melt the butter,
swirl the cream.
Let the salt of you
settle into the crevices
of his molars. His tongue
a bulge in the pocket
of his jaw, a tethered muscle
chasing a taste just out of
reach—a body
he doesn't own.

I take my responsibilities seriously
but I cannot overcome his stupidity
when he says *Black people always seem*   *happy.*
I am there when he walks you
by the water fountain,
his deep voice a seductive plea.
Tenderness when he dips his fingers
into churning waters, I part
his lips, tongue seeking to stir
caramel. You are never his jungle,
his dark continent to conquer,
but *my* high priestess to entreat.
If he wants melanin's cape to cover
his offspring, he must take down
your braids, grease your scalp.
When he peers into the burnished
amber of your eye, know that I
have bound and anointed him
with the dream of *caramel,*
he must kneel to honor it.

Prince Album Cover

With the lavender dreamscape behind him,
who was this god, naked astride a Pegasus?
I couldn't read the florid script, but didn't
need it to know love was feathered hair
framing a tan face, doe wide eyes, bare
thighs gripping a white-winged horse.
This nude body was not hidden like my father's
dirty magazines, so this meant art, an invitation
drawing my gaze close, closer to determine
where divinity nestled itself between man and horse.

Houses of the Holy Led Zeppelin Album Cover

In this temple of bare bottoms and breast buds,
my ears follow the steps of the guitar,
each chord progression a gospel raising
the hair on my arms. Is this what I am supposed
to feel in church? But it's Saturday and music
is exploding from the speakers in the living
room. *These white boys can rock,* Daddy says,
strumming baby sister's belly, her giddy laughter
an improvised solo. Spinning and twirling in this carpeted
pulpit, the whites of my father's eyes on fire,
sweat pouring down his face, reverb shaking the house,
I am spinning too, blessed by rock and roll.

A Black Woman Learns Ireland's History by Bus

It took a civil rights museum
to lift the skirts of the maiden
city of Derry. Here's where I saw
her Seamus Heaney tattoo.

Belfast, the stamp at
the bottom of the Titanic.
Here, I breathe in an industry
defined by ghosts,

then it's back to you, Dublin—
how I got sweet on you,
I do not know. Blame that
ancestor long ago—let's hope

it was consensual. But the
words that crawl your streets
align with my fault lines, neither
of us accustomed to joy.

On the road to Limerick,
crumbling forts shimmer
and shy away like mirages. On the river
Shannon, swans play their part

near King John's Castle.
Here Frederick Douglass honed
his pleas for justice. Shivers dart
down my bare brown arms.

But it's Newgrange where
stacked ancient stones call
my blood to rise. Two times a year
the sun flings a season's new song

into a quartz cavern. Here lifetimes
were spent, bent, building temples
to echo eons. At the entrance, water
collects in a giant rock's hollowed hand.

A wizened man whispers to me,
Dip your fingers and touch what ails you.

The First Gospel of Prince

Erotic City
Fingertips find the groove,
tap a rounding hip,
wake up to possibilities.

Girl
Boy, the word runs around
a mouth, whispering to the tongue
the hell it can raise with a flick.

Feel U Up
The curve, the heft,
a breast under palm;
consent is stiffening nipples.

Electric Intercourse
The air sears between hips, this melody
is a startled beauty—breathe in halting sips.

Vous êtes ici

*French for *you are here*

In a Paris museum, a cool blast lifts
her white cotton dress, billowing

round her cinnamon legs. *C'est Marilyn Monroe,*
says the man next to her. A smile

charms his laugh, she hastily smooths down
the unintended peep show.

Snapshot: Rain at the Rodin museum, sculptures glisten and glint.
Snapshot: Hotel room's plush velvet curtains, the color of spilled wine.

The hairy mound of a bush, framed,
elevated—*The Origin of the World.*

A Black woman molded in bronze,
shouldering Africa as *Four Parts of the World.*

Snapshot: A small café, a sip of coffee with cream, silk clouds slip down her
throat.
Snapshot: A perfumerie, discovering scents that will ghost her footsteps for
decades to come.

The best body is often retrospect.
She traveled over three thousand miles.

A man compared her to an icon—visibility
is more than being seen, it's not being

erased. On every map,
she remembers to look—

The Second Gospel of Prince

The Question of U
Divining answers from a guitar solo—
sycophant. Bare yourself to the speakers.

Sex
Hunger locked deep within her. The key,
a man's tender inquisition. Let him touch her
and see what insatiable can bear.

Shockadelica
A drum kick
knocks the door down,
the guitar solo greedily
laps the air.

Rock Hard in a Funky Place
His falsetto loosening
the screws of the speakers.

The Goddess of Lust

I Wonder U
—PRINCE

Lust exists as lingering musk,
Want's erotic cousin.
She puckers for the kiss
but does not blow it, letting
the tension grow—
imagination deepening
the blush. The fermented
ardor of daydreams
keeps her tipsy, never drunk.
Lust sings of impulse
to the nerves—
here, ache
quivers as a verb.

To Lust, flirtation is
a mansion, sexual tension
a wide, circular driveway.
Those are Lust's fingers
curled on the poker,
stoking the flames.
Lust spit shines her things:
soaked panties, stiff jeans.
She is the prize thighs quake for
when clits are rubbed raw,
for her yearning is an oiled frame.
Let loose desire,
a damp sheet's stain.
Lust is the fire gasping,
Lust burns her name.

Her 21st Summer

She hangs out in shadows
      contours musk-
scented and slick.
      Such supple skin
leaves a body teetering
      between infatuation
and ruin, playing men
      with house money.

A winter before,
      one man held her,
broke her, and by summer,
      Lake Erie, sea breezes,
handsome-faced men,
      a bed, a boat; a girl thought
she had put herself
      back together again.

Biology-honed weapons,
      a waist to match her age.
Five different belly chains.
      Look Ma, no bra, look Dad, no slip,
figure so slight
      she's a one-handed grip.

Walk into a bar, no wallet,
      only the small of her back
talking, looking for a hand
      to guide it home.
She thought she was back
      together again.

Trusting a lover
    for the sake of the night,
she swallows what's set out—
    Buttery Nipple, Grasshopper,
Long Island Iced Tea;
    the wet ring on the empty
bar winks back,
    ice melting indolently;
midnight comes into heat.

    His arms guide her to his Jeep.
The sheer thrill of flight,
    top down, quarter moon of light
speed-kissed air whipping past;
    maybe there is a granite cliff,
a side girlfriend, slick pavement;
    maybe she hits it.
Maybe she misses.

The Third Gospel of Prince

Irresistible Bitch
He's never known
her taste mingled with his.

Joy in Repetition
Is the alchemy of want
powerful enough to disrupt time
and displace space?—fingers hover.

We Can Funk (Jewel Box Version)
I could worship the taste of you.
Just close the door.

The Goddess of Idolatry

Swear by thy gracious self / Which is the god of my idolatry
—JULIET, *ROMEO AND JULIET*

1
Go to him bare,
he loves these *Noon Rendezvous.*

2
Incant the lyrics to *When2RinLove,*
cultivate lightning strikes
between your thighs

3
Be his Gemini—find your Camille.
Let *Shockadelica* make you squeal.
Let him plead and twirl his way
into your pants, court heartbreak
for just one night with his face.
Purple Electricity, flowers littered
on a white floor, do it in the limousine,
tonight, live the fantasy,
bubble bath, pants on.

4
Purify yourself in Lake Minnetonka,
be his sinner without care.
Invoke *Erotic City,* make it come alive,
taste his hot flash of animal lust,
fingers dipping up and down,
in and out, around your lake.
Become *Delirious,* bring *Pandemonium,*
and since *Gigolos Get Lonely Too,*
make yourself free for a couple of hours,
maybe the next seven years. Always be in his hair.

5

Every Friday night
his music is his body
in remembrance of him.
Take it inside you.

6

Make your love shout.

7 (April)

Let the rain come,
17 days, 17 long nights.

Gold

Dig the picture,
purple tulips and lilacs,
wilting after a tempest,
then drink the overflow.

Love Letter

Dear T, age 16

You buy *The Illustrated Love Letters* by Lady Antonia Fraser at Trover's,
the Marquis de Sade's *120 Days of Sodom* at a Georgetown sex shop.
When you know next to nothing about a subject, you research it.

Sade's lurid details first excite then numb you. Page after page
of Fraser's love letters encase your romantic stance in silk;
then there's the sketch of Keats on his death bed. You swoon,

wooed. Your eyes memorize the cream background:
sensuous pencil strokes, the poet's full lips, slightly
parted, broken by his last sigh.

Dear T, age 23

On the first night you sleep with your future husband
you wake, startled by the moonlight's bright face.
It spills between slanted blinds, graces his pale

profile, slides down his nose, lands at a bowed mouth,
a pretty pink pout. Memory slips back to Keats.
You must be dreaming. You reach over—touch

his shoulder. You do this the next time, the next, next.
Sometimes he stirs, sometimes he sleeps through your quiet
astonishment, your sated fingertips, your longing, your glee.

Dear T, age 43

Twenty years later, surprise still wakes you to a smooth shoulder.
The moonlight, gleaming a full-size, how real he is to your
petite frame, his seeping warmth a beloved refrain.

"Don't Disturb This Groove"

after The System and Galway, Ireland

Even with Galway beckoning,
your kiss mixed with last night's wine
was too intoxicating. If I could be
this wanton and beautiful in your eyes,
then let your hands find hollows slick
with glee, let your mouth meet mine
between words, kissing sentences,
tongues diagramming intention. Let the
mirror frame the sight of our worn bodies
reflecting a youthful, tempered energy. Let
plans of tours and walks be replaced by
clenched bedsheets, music masking moans,
the surprise of ardor as swift and intense
as lightning. Let our skin be framed in a slant
of sunlight, sudden and sweet. Let us find not
sleep at Nox hotel but never-ending bounty—
breakfast of black pudding, bangers, and tea.
Let the cab driver's Irish music of an accent
greet us open and free. The stiff, cold Atlantic wind
trying, and failing, to steal our burnished glow.

Ode to Orgasms

When the wild abandonment
of pleasure calls, trilling its
glorious song, you surrender,

forget yourself,
respond in kind, moaning
an ecstatic ode

to the rivers of flesh—
the delta,
the well-plowed field.

This back-arching work
results in trembling limbs,
shuddering, simpering joy.

Not all is submission.
You sought this treasured bird.
Whether in sun-dappled beds,

sudden on a Saturday,
while children frolic a floor below,
or on a sodden tree trunk

in the aftermath of a February's
record-breaking snow.
Be it a quick tryst

in a hotel stairwell, desire
domineering a long drive—
you committed, flung open

the shutters of propriety
to pursue this elusive creature.
Now grasp its golden tail feathers,

leap from mountaintop
to mountaintop, gulp
that sweet, sweet, fleeting air.

Slow Drag

after "Dancing in the Dark" by Cannonball Adderly

With a leisurely tease, the saxophone ascends
a soft whisper, almost too low to hear. A timbre
vibrates the inner ear, Blakely's drum dances to a sigh,
tremors race down the nerves' tangled rope.

The spaghetti strap of her cocktail dress slips off
her shoulder. Her stocking feet whisper their two-
step on the carpet's short-looped hush. Her dark
curls spring and fall from their pent-up grace,

sketching themselves on the nape of her neck,
beckoning his fingertips or lips to follow. Her
Manhattan drained, glass angled dangerously
in her hand, a swollen cherry tempted to fall out

and stain the night. Her husband slouches into
the hollows of her neck, led there by the bare traces
of her perfume. Their bodies heavy with the weight
of work. What feels better than this measured

surrender? Letting the music lead them through
the well-worn paces of love, coasting on what's left
of the day's energy to linger, limpid and luxuriously
into this slow drag.

Escape Ladder

The dead end
nights of it,
too tired for it,
a kiss ends it,
he turns on his side,
you sleep on it.

Oh, the *pull*, the pull
of the black hole of wonder.
Imagine your own consumption.
Reckless lips, a new lover,
the island dew of you,
sweat over sinew.

Pick a man, far from your fingertips—
Scotch-tape his *Tiger Beat* picture
in your mind's locker. A crush is just
a way to re-engorge the soft tissues
of want, help the sun sprint the sky—
chariot wheels greased by lust, Apollo's cheeks
peeking under a loose chiton.

Part III

The Goddess of Anger

Did he touch you?
Did he hit you?
With jagged words,
or closed fist?
Did he laugh at you?
Were you polite even
then—were you lava
under the skin? Then,
let me in. Unsheathe
the dagger of me.
You've tasted pain,
now let me master it.
Let me in. I'll use
the dust of his bones
for tea. I'll rise, vengeful
and caustic, a florid fury
steeped in seething,
I'll make his eyes bleed.
Let me in. I'll dissect him,
unflinchingly, a backhand
slap, a rake of fingernails—
I'll spit my small mercies.
I'll dance on him in stilettos,
paint my toenails OPI red
while the blood congeals.
Let me be your ignition point,
your pitch, the whoosh
of hot, sweet breath.
I'm all your swallowed heat
simmered into flesh.
I, too, can lift burdens.
Let go of fear, of retribution.
Let go of decorum and shame.
Ride Rage until it bucks

then jump on it again.
Damn it, let me, let me,
Let. Me. In.

Lola Visits the Underworld

Lola did what Orpheus couldn't—
she snatched her big Sister straight from hell.

Folks say the war changed Sis's man
but he wasn't no dummy before.
He came from this shit, putting
hands on women. The first time

he hit Sis, Lola was little, maybe seven,
maybe six. She balled up her tiny fist
and punched him in the back—called
her brothers, sisters, *sorry bastards*

for not backing her up. There was another
time he hit and another, until the day came
he put Sis in the hospital. A metal plate

in her head, stitches where the knife cut.
For seven days she was a shade of herself.
When she finally walked out,
Lola was right there next to Sis's man.

Baby sis Betty came for backup. Four
of them in the car. Ride ain't never been
quieter. Sis's man dropped them home
on his way to work. His heel barely left

the doorsill when the sisters pulled suitcases out.
The bus ride North was long.
Once, twice, Sis said she thought about
going back. But Lola told her, *Sis, don't*

look back. Don't ever look back. She never did.
That fool Orpheus could learn something.

Backup (An Ode to Weathering)

for Arline Geronimus

Mix ancestral and everyday trauma, African call,
American response. Drum it on tight tendons,
skin, suffused and shiny, soft tissues singing of
soreness, observing it like a holiday. (It's just Tuesday.)
Speed it up 7.5 times, let blood pressure reach the high notes,
diabetes, the low ones. Let obesity morbidly thump

the bass lines, while glycogen's fight-or-flight hit
the high hat. Isn't each day, each step outside in America
a scream? Listen to the resounding soundtrack:
You Don't Belong Here, Go Back to Africa and that original hit *Nigger!*
—always number one with a bullet. When the school's White

gaze singles out your son, implore adrenaline and cortisol
to slow their ragged runs. When applying for a mortgage with a
lower interest rate, after the next White businessman
lets the door slam in your face, tell this body not to hum its fate—

fear, anxiety, and chronic depression, the constant refrain.
Inflammation as the blood races to the mic *again* and *again*.
Measure one, discrimination, maternal mortality, measure two

heart disease, socioeconomic conditions, tune up the fibroids,
open up the throat, dig down, hold that note. Black women know

how to sing backup. Our pain always in perfect pitch.

When I Am the Only One in the Room

The Southern roots of *y'all*
makes music in my mouth's map.

In the North I cuff the C hard for *couplet*
then soften it for *child* and *chain*.

When *bookin'* I drop the *g*—
depending on the audience,

I find it again running. By ten
I knew when to let the *W* whistle

in *whom* but darken the room
for the *D* to fall asleep

in *I un't know nothin'* but the beauty
of when a double negative will do,

how to make this English buck
then soft shoe when I see you.

The Goddess of Cleaning

I bequeath you bleach,
its singeing sting.
I bequeath you the scrub
brush, best done on hands
and knees. I bequeath you
ammonia for the exorcism
of dirt. I bequeath you power
over clutter—the washing
machine's spin, the dryer's
lint grin. I bequeath you
the salvation of sweeping
—a consecrated grip on
the broomstick. I bequeath
you the dustpan's collection
plate, the floor's sanctified
echo, the trash bin's penitent
face. I bequeath you the
gospel of a mop, the sacred
slosh of a rinse bucket's
second coming. I bequeath
you the torn T-shirt as rag,
the two-sided sponge,
vinegar and newspaper's
squeak, the glass free
of streak. I bequeath you
an old toothbrush for tiles'
hard-to-reach grime.
I bequeath you the grunt
and scrub of wool,
the eradication of rust.
Trust in me, I baptize you
in sweat, labor's beatific
stain. I bequeath you
the power to change
one room at a time.

Partus sequitur ventrem

A Latin phrase that stands for the principle that the children of an enslaved woman are themselves born as slaves and owned by their mother's master.

I. MORNING

His knobby six-year-old knees,
his anxious pace as if to keep step
with the questions' steady overflow:
"Is there a giant octopus in the Bermuda Triangle?"
"How is paper made?"
"How do fireworks know when to explode?"
No one told me Black boys could burn
so bright. Wait, I am wrong, the dark sky
has seen their fire snuffed by white hoods,
malevolent blue eyes in bluer uniforms,
White women's screams—all have been match
to their tinder wood. So I hug my son tight.
Kiss the curl cropped so close it's straight.
My mother-eye insatiable, he is dessert
and I'll always have seconds. Each morning
I lick my thumb, clean him up good, wishing
in vain the amniotic sac had dried to armor.

II. NIGHT

His lisp, loose, syrupy-sweet,
sneaks into my ear. Feel its heat,
small source more flicker than
flame, flanked by arms still
dreaming of muscle. He claims
my squishy stomach *the best pillow.*
If the security of our locked arms

could extend beyond growth spurts,
clocks, calendars, to the someone
interviewing him, to the someone
following him in the store, to the
someone holding my son's life
in trembling fingers poised above
a phone's keypads—let my love
be a note safety-pinned to his chest
—*send him back alive, unharmed.*
As a Black mother in America,
I know my wails are birthright,
pinned with iron,
penned in ink.

The Account of Katie Mae

For my grandmother 9/9/1926–7/26/2019

We the People
3/5 of a person

in Order to form a more perfect Union
When Ann started school
they closed it;
rather than have Black kids go
it was closed
for two years

establish Justice
I was working at this cafeteria
It was all White
the manager
came in the back
and said, "Don't send any food out"
we didn't know
what it was about
they wouldn't let us
serve food   it was a sit-in
after   he closed that cafeteria
closed it period
I thought
why do people hate us so bad?
so bad you won't give us a little food
or don't want us to sit down?
or even close your cafeteria
on account of we want to eat?

insure Domestic Tranquility
We made our dolls
from the flour sack

burlap
picture of a pretty blonde girl
we stuffed her
with cotton

provide for the common defence
The way my father told me
we had land in Georgia
'til the Klan
ran us off it

promote the general Welfare
My brother died
when he was ten-year-old
he was real smart
but he got sick
you had to go miles
and miles to get to a hospital
thinking after I was grown up
if he had gone to a hospital
he would've lived

and secure the Blessings of Liberty to ourselves and our Posterity
I worked on the farm
picked cotton
as soon as I could get out there
as late as I could stay
sunrise to sundown
and you want to be out
early before it gets so hot
cuz the sun
beaming down on you all day
is more than a notion
the farm we worked on
was a half and half

whatever you have
half of it goes to the man
that owned the farm
the next one to you
that was your payment

**do ordain and establish this Constitution for the United States of
America**

The Goddess of the South

I'm Ma'am-ma telling you the best way to rid them pimples
was to wash your face with fresh morning urine.
I'm there when ya' momma teaches you how to pick
chitlins'—small fingers finding bits of straw and bone
until a full bucket cooks down to one plate. I was in your
mother's hand as she rounded your head as a baby,
dem soft spots shifting into the curve of her palm. I'm sugar,
baking soda, cornmeal, and the cast iron skillet when your
great aunt shows you how to make cornbread from scratch.
I'm every bite of peach cobbler you sneak even though you
allergic to peaches. 'Member how you ain't know
Bessemah was Bessemer until a road trip to Atlanta
brought you in shoutin' distance of Alabama?
Or Auntie Surley's real name was Sara Lee, how I dragged
your Northern tongue, taught it to linger in the soft vowels,
the syrup of me thick like Alaga in your mouth. I'm in every
shotgun story you know, like that time you and your sister
heard that rattle when y'all was playing in the tall grass near
Aunty Surley's juke joint? Umhmm, how matter of fact
and fluid that big woman was, putting a plate
of freshly fried chicken in front of y'all with one hand,
grabbing her shotgun with the other, and kept it stepping.
But I evolve too, baby, my young preachers
keep me so fresh and so clean. I gleam in the grits you pour
butter, and yes, sugah, because I do as you do, my beautiful
brown children, when you spread to California, Wisconsin,
New York, Illinois, and Ohio you take me with you.
You make neckbones—teach your children how to work
hard for such sweet little meat, you cut rabbit chunks
into your oxtail soup, you house the children of this cousin,
that daughter, this sister, and raise them as your own,
arms always extended in a net of family, of blood. How I
groomed you child, let you overhear 'she ain't got a pot
to piss in nor a window to throw it out of' and 'what you
get in the giddy-up is what you get in the round-up.'

I'm always at yo' table, the hot sauce you want on Friday's
fried fish, that hankering for smothered pork chops
you get on dreary November days. I lecture you in your sleep,
when a shuttering of past relatives show up, you wake
knowing it's been a visitation. (If you tell yo' momma,
she gon' reach for the Numbers book.) I keep one of your
feet planted firmly in my red clay, be it Little Rock,
Pine Bluff or Crisp County, Georgia. With honeyed names
like Nae, Cousin Peaches, Grease, Junebug, I keep your mind
running in circles, connecting blood to family, friends, and back.
Baby gurl, you'll never be free of me, all the black bodies
I've consumed? Yalls blood makes the soil shine. The roots
of your family tree may shift so some of the dirt falls across
the Mason Dixon line but I will always claim you as mine, mine, mine.
If you ever change your mind, about leaving, leaving me behind . . .

Thank You Jesus

When the blue and red sirens pass you,
when the school calls because your child
beat the exam and not a classmate,
when the smartphone drops but does not crack,
the rush escaping your mouth betrays your upbringing:
thank you Jesus—a balm over the wound.
When the mammogram finds only density,
when the playground tumble results
in a bruise, not a broken bone,
like steam from a hot teakettle
thank you Jesus—and the pent-up fear
vents upward, out. Maybe it's a hand
over breast, supplication learned deeper
than flesh as if one could shush the soul,
the fluttering heartbeat with three words.
Maybe it's not so dire—an almost trip on the sidewalk,
the accumulated sales total showing savings upon savings,
maybe it's as small as an empty seat on the Metro
or maybe *thank you Jesus*—becomes the refrain
every time your husband pulls into the driveway,
alive and whole, and no one has mistaken him
for all the black, scary things. You mutter it,
helpless to stop yourself from the invocation
of a grandmother who gave you your first bible,
you say it because your mother, even knowing
your doubt as a vested commodity, still urges prayer.
You learned early to cast the net—*thank you Jesus*
and it's a sweet needle that gathers the fraying thread,
hemming security in steady stitches. From birth
you've heard this language; as an adult
you've seen religion used nakedly as ambition, yet
this sacrifice of praise still slips past your lips,
this lyrical martyr of your dying faith.

Crescendo

My son nests—pawing
each pillow like a breast
fleshed out and so newly
forgotten. I've spanked him

once tonight. He takes turns
laughing, then crying, defiant,
then hungry. In his mouth
my name—all need. Pursed

lips plead, *Mommy* and I
am guilty of the same sin.
I miss his curled and tucked
weight. Embryo, the deepest

root yanked clean. This is why
babies are born crying
into this world, having held
fast to such an intimate tether;

who willingly would let go again?
But today another White cop walked
free, another Black body was still
on the ground. "Not indicted"

undoubtedly the future outcome.
Four years ago, I crossed labor's
red sea of pain to birth a boy—
no doctor hit his backside, now I raise

my hand to complete an act
older than me, breaking the black
back of the boy to make a man
who can survive in America.

Mommy he calls me and my teats
threaten to weep old milk at our stasis.
Both of us needing the succor of sleep,
both us fighting—him, to keep me near

me, punishing him to be left alone.
He crawls into my lap, his heart
is three, his body, a lanky four.
I cover him with a blanket

too thin to mean it. We rock
on the edge of his bed. Listening
to the symphony's fourth movement:
the crescendo sweet, full of tension,

violin strings singing. I think
Mozart must have known something
of loving with such a tender fear
that it breaks you open like a welt

that bleeds to heal. Tonight, I give up,
cuddling this boy so full of belief
in himself, I'm too tired with love
to beat it out of him.

This Poem Suggests Revolution

This poem no longer consents to play
mammy or to wet nurse a seething rage
at her own black teat. America, your teeth
have come in—you nip too much. This poem

refuses to play religion, a bible verse will not
absolve you, America. If the pursuit of happiness,
life, and liberty came from the creator, she is
about ready to backhand you in the face.

This poem will not be your bottom bitch,
America. This poem does not consent to
Blackness being window-dressing for the
diversity brochure of a country where

the board of directors never changed.
This poem reads the fine print on you,
America. This poem consents to be:
black ink, a clenched fist, pepper spray,

and black soles marching on asphalt—
freedom for **and** from you, America.
If need be, this poem consents to double
as witness—the dotted *i* in the missing

reparations decree. Until then, let this poem
heckle you, America. Let it yell *goddamn US,
choke on cotton,* while fanning itself and the
flames. Understand, this poem doesn't

want to be bloodthirsty; it would rather
write about the cleanse of a cloud burst
than the vengeful force of a water hose.
In truth, this poem courts hope. Like a volta,

it wants to turn the page, writing: *America,*
let us pen a new document. Not a perpetual union
but a chokehold removed — as a Black throat breathing
freely is a self-evident truth — let these lines be facts

submitted to a candid world. And this poem,
when spoken or read, let it alter, let it abolish you.

a more perfect Union

Dear America,

When I say America,
I mean, White people.
You need a new name.
I respectfully decline
to continue this narrative.
Evolution is upon us,
like a kiss, my tongue twists
—I'm getting sick from
holding it *Massa, Officer*
—with you, fear is always
a whip, or White lady
calling 911. We grew up
in the same house: cotton
fields, colonial red bricks,
plantation shutters. But in 2016,
you shit the bed. Since then,
my blues smoke,
spirits singe my throat;
oblivion's a better dance partner,
at least with her I cough,
but don't choke. Under
your patriotic blanket lies
a thorny bouquet. You market
it well, so I miss the smell
of copper, blood steady seeping
down my wrist. The Founding
Fathers bought bodies
but everyday *I'm* the one
asked for receipts. I breastfed
the beast, 'til it gnashed
and took off running on its feet.
Can I get store credit for my rage?
A trade-in voucher for heartbreak?

I'm not a White man with a gun.
I can't shoot up a school, church,
or movie theater for Burger King,
a little right wing fun.
America, are you listening?

You need a new name.
I cannot keep talking *to* myself
when I am not talking *about* myself.
Maybe America isn't who
I need to talk to.

Dear Reader,

We need to knuckle-up.
From old newspapers
to online news, head-
lines excusing Whiteness
ain't failed to disappoint
me yet. It's time for the remix.
Let the masses DJ, not another
oligarchy set; be that more perfect
Union. And while the ink is still wet,
make capitalism beg for forgiveness,
forgive college debt, establish a general
income, make felons voting legit,
write in healthcare—not that Western
mindset but holistic (mediate on that).

Dear Reader,

I need you to know
I have hope in us yet.

Notes

"Vous êtes ici" references Gustave Courbet's *The Origin of the World* and Jean-Baptiste Carpeaux's *The Four Parts of the World Holding the Celestial Sphere,* both on display at the Musée d'Orsay in Paris, France.

"The First, Second, and Third Gospels of Prince" use the titles of his many B-sides as headings.

"The Account of Katie Mae" uses lines from the Preamble to the Constitution and language from oral accounts from my maternal grandmother, Katie Mae Conway York.

"The Goddess of the South" uses a line from Sam Cooke's "Bring It On Home to Me."

"This Poem Suggests Revolution" uses language from the Declaration of Independence.

"a more perfect Union" takes its title from the Preamble to the Constitution.

The *Journal* Charles B. Wheeler Poetry Prize

a more perfect Union
TERI ELLEN CROSS DAVIS

Praying Naked
KATIE CONDON

Lethal Theater
SUSANNAH NEVISON

Radioapocrypha
BK FISCHER

June in Eden
ROSALIE MOFFETT

Somewhere in Space
TALVIKKI ANSEL

The River Won't Hold You
KARIN GOTTSHALL

Antidote
COREY VAN LANDINGHAM

Fair Copy
REBECCA HAZELTON

Blood Prism
EDWARD HAWORTH HOEPPNER

Men as Trees Walking
KEVIN HONOLD

American Husband
KARY WAYSON

Shadeland
ANDREW GRACE

Empire Burlesque
MARK SVENVOLD

Innocence
JEAN NORDHAUS

Autumn Road
BRIAN SWANN

Spot in the Dark
BETH GYLYS

Writing Letters for the Blind
GARY FINCKE

Mechanical Cluster
PATTY SEYBURN

Magical Thinking
JOSEPH DUEMER

Stone Sky Lifting
LIA PURPURA

Captivity Narrative
MARY ANN SAMYN

Blessings the Body Gave
WALT McDONALD

Anatomy, Errata
JUDITH HALL

Stones Don't Float: Poems Selected and New
JOHN HAAG

Crossing the Snow Bridge
FATIMA LIM-WILSON

The Creation
BRUCE BEASLEY

Night Thoughts and Henry Vaughan
DAVID YOUNG

History as a Second Language
DIONISIO D. MARTINEZ

Guests
TERESA CADER

Rooms, Which Were People
MARY CROSS

The Book of Winter
SUE OWEN

Life-list
ROBERT CORDING

Popular Culture
ALBERT GOLDBARTH